The Walking Lord Shiva of Varanasi

The Journey of Avdhoot Trailanga Swami

Tulika Singh

Illustrated by

Anamika Pal

Delta Book World
New Delhi - 110002

Disclaimer

While the author doesn't make any claims for the fool proof authenticity of all facts and timelines, intention of the book is to introduce Avdhoot Trailanga Swami and his history to the readers in a fun and light manner.

Requests for permission should be addressed to

mail@ashwathatreebooks.com

Find more of similar books on www.ashwathatreebooks.com

First Published in 2026
ISBN : 978-93-85719-36-3

Published by **Abhishek Goel** on behalf of

Delta Book World
G-4, Prahlad House
4832/24, Ansari Road
New Delhi - 110 002 (India)

Ph. : 011- 4707 2321
E-mail : deltabookworld@gmail.com

PRINTED IN INDIA

"Those who forget their own nature, their Godly essence, forget the power within themselves. Our real nature most often is mistaken by others. They prefer to believe in a miracle of the supernatural, rather than the inner strength of the powers that all of us possess."

Trailanga Swami

In Telangana region of Andhra Pradesh, there lived a pious and noble couple Narshimha Rao and Bidyabati Devi. Both being great devotees of Lord Shiva, often spent their time in devotional service and community work. Narsimha Rao was a wealthy landlord with extensive land and property coupled with a loving heart.

He loved Bidyapati Devi who was a chaste and a loving wife, and one who supported her husband in all his endeavours.

Many happy years of their married life had been spent in each other companionship and service of lord, but there was one void in their life which made them feel incomplete.

Their hearts ached when they saw happy giggling faces of little children as it reminded them of their own empty nest.

Thoughts of being childless and anxieties about the future gave Bidyabati sleepless nights. She begged god to fulfill her wishes, but in vain. Time passed and with little hope on their side, Bidyabati forced her husband to marry once more for progeny.

Unwillingly but finally agreeing Narsimha Rao got married again, but only few months had passed and Bidyabati Devi one day found out that she was pregnant, finally. After protecting young baby in the womb, and enriching him with her love and blessings, Bidyavati Devi gave birth to a beautiful baby after nine months.

They named him Shivrama.

As a young boy, Shivrama always accompanied his mother to the temples and other holy services. Tagging to her sari, Shivrama spent most of his time under the shade of his mother's love. Bidyavati who had waited too long for a child would pour out her heart and soul to little Shivrama, who took great interest in learning devotional songs and chants, for Lord Shiva.

When alone, he would often be seen lost in thoughts, staring blank into the air, or with closed eyes meditating for hours. His favourite spots were his home temple where the family had installed a Shiv Linga and an idol of Mahakali.

One day while Bidyabati was into deep trance and young Shivrama had dozed off on her lap, she was shaken to an vivid experience where she saw a bright light emanating out of Shiv lingam and entering her son's body. This and many more such events made Bidyabati reiterate that an evolved soul had taken birth through her.

As Shivram grew up, he became further quiet and introspective, he was fast losing all interests in the ways of the social acts and living. His parents specially his father thought that marriage could be good for him as it would bring brightness to his colourless life and he will start getting interested in the ways of the world.

Shivram blatantly refused, as he saw marriage as an impediment to his spiritual life. Ultimately Narsimha Rao gave up his wish of marrying Shivram and prepared to marry the younger son instead, who would carry his name forward in all societal purposes.

Time passed, and one day Narsimha Rao also left for heavenly abode. After the final rituals and prayers, Shivram expressed his burning wish to leave home and take up religious life to his mother.

Grief-stricken Bidyabati Devi couldn't let his only son leave him then when she herself was getting over her husband's death. She vowed him to stay back and leave only after she had left for the holy abode.

She promised him that if he would stay with her until her death, he will surely find the highest blessings and ultimate liberation. Shivrama agreed to his mother and stayed back.

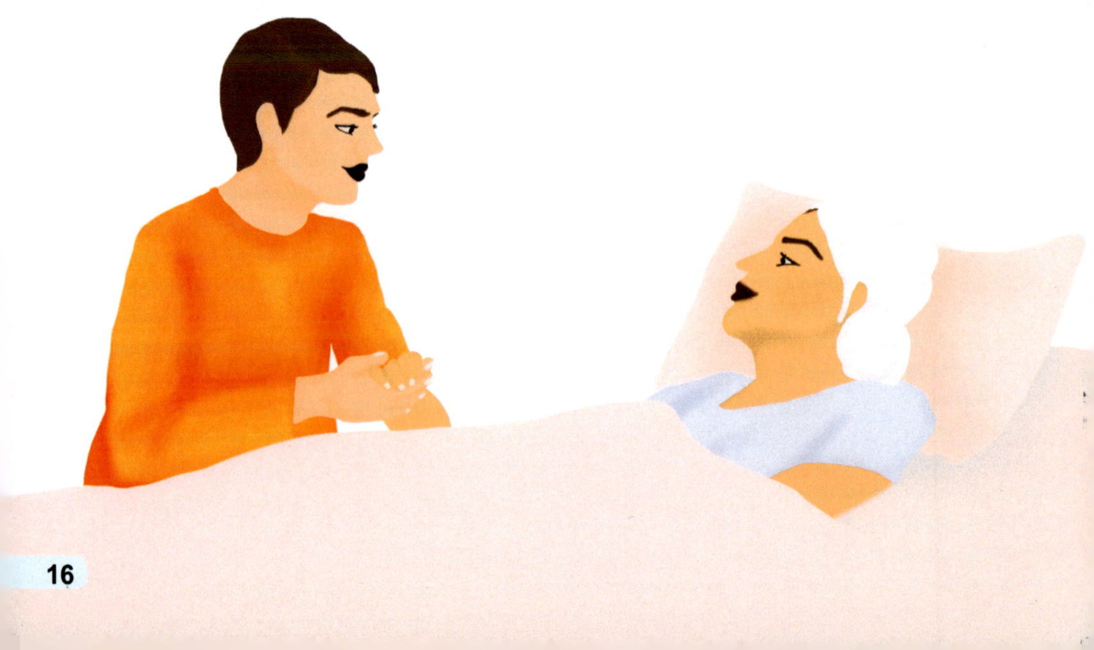

Some years later when his mother died, his last attachment to the world was broken and it brought finality to Shivrama's decision to leave the world and live like a Sanyasi.

After offering his mother's earthly body to the fire, Shivrama kept on staring at the burning embers till late in the evening, thinking of impermanence of the human life.

For many days, Shivrama stayed at the cremation ground, weeping, laughing and pondering. Everyday many dead bodies were burnt in front of him and he would stare at them blankly, then he would suddenly get up and rub the warm ash all around his body and run around like a mendicant.

His brother and his relatives coaxed him many times to return home and live a normal life but to no avail. Shivrama stayed at the cremation ground for many years, and slowly gave up on proper clothes, food and home. He would sit motionless for days and one day left the place without informing anyone.

He roamed in the plains and in the lofty mountains of Himalayas calling for the divine and looking for a master who could take him to the next level of his spiritual practice. In harshest of winters, he would walk barefoot meeting rishis and sadhus staying in various caves in the mountains.

After many years of futile searching and wandering one day he reached a stony cave, where he sat down to rest a bit. The place was overlooking a deep valley with glaciers around it.

Shivrama was heartbroken and disappointed by now in his inability to find a master who could show him the path forward.

In his desperation he called out to the lord in his loud Voice 'Are you there?'

The valley echoed Are you there, Are you there, Are you there…??

or

'You are not there'

The valley echoed Are you there, Are you there

then

You are not there, You are not there….

Watery eyed Shivrama now burst into tears, the echoing valley, had given him a simple answer of the ever-existing god. It's our faith he understood is the key, if we believe god is there, we will feel his presence in everything around and if we think he is not there then we will miss seeing his presence.

Not many minutes had passed, Shivrama heard a soothing voice call his name.

Shivrama, Shivrama aho you have come!

I have been waiting for you so long.

Not seeing anyone around, Shivrama got up from the stone and walked a few steps towards the voice which was calling him, within 20 minutes he saw a cave going down in the ground and he started walking towards it, on entering the tunnel like structure and after walking few steps Shivrama found a saint radiating with light and energy poised on a raised stone.

"Happy to see you, Shivrama."

"The almighty is very pleased with you."

"I have been ordained to give you some spiritual practices which will help you grow further in your journey, come sit near me" said the saint.

This was Swami Bhagirathananda who initiated Shivaram into his monkhood and gave him the new name of Swami Ganapati Saraswathi.

Under the tutelage of a realized the master, Shivrama now Swami Ganpati shone like a diamond. He reached the pinnacle of his search and learning and spent around ten years in the loving presence of his guru.

Later Swami Ganapati Saraswathi, popularly came to be known as Trailanga Swami. (referencing the fact that he spoke Telugu and was from Andhra Pradesh).

After acquiring many spiritual powers and his guru's demise, Trailanga Swami left for long pilgrimages to holy places such as Varanasi, Mansarovar and Rameswaram as advised by his master.

Trailanga Swami had Ashtsiddhis by divine grace, meaning he had super powers to Reduce or expand his body to very small size (Laghima and Mahima) he could go anywhere (Pratpti), make any wish come true (Prakyma), control five elements (Vashitva) and many such powers which came to him.

Once while he walked in the plains, he met a woman weeping over her dead son, bitten by a poisonous snake.

On seeing a yogi like demeanor, the women begged Trailanga Swami to bring his son back to life. Swami unaware of his newly acquired powers asked about the snake and called it out. Soon everyone saw a big black snake come wriggling to the dead boy and touch it. Miraculously the boy came back to life and stood up in minutes. Everyone gathered around started in amazement and bowed down to the Swami.

Of all the tirthas he stayed longest at Kashi and would roam the streets of the city as an avdhoot.

One interesting anecdote is that once there was a severe storm and heavy rains were lashing the river Ganga. Swami ran to the banks and started looking for something, but after some persuasion told one of his devotee that he was waiting there to save a boat which would soon going to sink. Within no time two boats appeared on the horizon, swayed by the heavy winds and they both toppled and went in the water with the pilgrims onboard.

Trailanga Swami disappeared from the banks and in a few minutes the boat came on the shore with all the people aboard intact and off course Swami. No one except the devotee realized that it was all because of the grace of the saint.

The Swami was consistently seen to drink deadly poisons and remain unaffected by it. Once, some of the disbeliever wanted to declare Trailanga Swami as a scam. In this order they brought a bucket full with the calcium lime mixture. Telang Swami drank the full bucket without any ill effect, but the men ended with terrible stomach ache. Then he broke his natural silence in order to clarify the law of karma, its reason and effect.

Around the year 1701, Trailanga Swami moved to Nepal for doing some spiritual practices. One day while he was sitting under a large tree, a roaring lion came running and took refuge near him, Swami patted him and caressed his mane to comfort him. Following him, soon came the King of Nepal who was out hunting for animals and this Lion was his target. The King and his men were astonished to see a wild beast sitting like a tamed pet near a sage.

Trailanga Swami admonished the King that if he didn't have the capacity to grant a life to any being, he also didn't have the right to kill anyone. They all bowed down their heads in shame.

The King understood the greatness of the realized saint and later went back with precious gifts and jewels. But Trailanga Swami refused all, saying they were all useless for a Sanyasi.

It's in Varanasi, where he settled down for most period of his life. Trailanga Swami was a tall and heavy weight man, with a big pot belly. He weighed approximately 140 kg even though he ate proper food rarely. He never cooked or begged for food and sustained on whatever came his way.

Swami was always in an exalted state of knowledge with no body-consciousness in him. He lived like a Avdhoot and would often wander around in the streets of Varanasi naked.

The harassed police of Banaras came to regard him as a baffling problem child. The natural Swami was unaware of his stark nakedness but the police wasn't and they would put him in jail for not wearing clothes. While in the jail cell, with guard still on duty, Swami would disappear from the cell and be found walking on the roof of the building. He would appear and disappear on his own accord and baffle the police officers.

Thousands of people have seen Trailanga Swami floating on the Ganges for days on end or remaining hidden under the waves for hours too. Frequently he was seen during Indian summer days the sand would became so hot that no one could set foot on it. But Swami lay comfortably on it, without any ill effects.

The Story goes that once the great Bengali saint Ramakrishna Paramhans came to Varanasi and met Trailanga Swami. Both of them were so happy to be with each other and spoke only in silence. Ramkrishna showed his interest to visit the Kashi Vishwanath temple, but as time was running out, he concluded it might not be possible. As he thought this and turn around to leave, there stood, instead of Swami, Lord Vishwanath himself.

After this sighting, Ramakrishna said that even though, Trailanga Swami had taken a body but he was truly the "The Walking Lord Shiva of Varanasi ".

Once while, Trailanga Swami was praying to Ma Kali, she instructed him to dive into Ganga and get something for her. Soon everyone saw Swami ji dive into the waters and come back with a huge boulder, shaped as a Shivalinga under his arm pit. Later this Shivlinga was placed at the temple and it was named as Trailangeshwar.

Trailanga Swami had announced beforehand the day of his departure and had instructed his followers to make a wooden box for his dead body, and immerse it in holy Ganga after his demise. A day before his death, he sat motionless like a statue. Devotees offered water to him as an abhisheka from early morning till noon as a living form of the Lord Shiva.

At the moment of his demise, thousands who had gathered there saw a huge beam of divine light in the sky. The big wooden box sank and came up empty.

The year was 1881.

Such is the presence of these great saints, that even today as we walk in the narrow lanes of Benaras, towards his temple which houses his samadhi, we can feel his divine presence and his abundant grace.